The
Truth
About
Christmas

The
Truth
About
Christmas

By
Santa Claus

A Crossroad Book
The Crossroad Publishing Company
New York

1997

The Crossroad Publishing Company
370 Lexington Avenue, New York, NY 10017

Printed in the United States of America

Library of Congress Cataloging-in-Publication Data
Santa Claus.
    The truth about Christmas / Santa Claus.
        p.   cm.
    ISBN 0-8245-1678-8
    1. Christmas – Meditations.   I. Title.
BV45.S314   1997
242'.335 – dc21   97-8902
                                                   CIP

Contents

Introduction

Why I Wrote This Book

EAR FRIEND AND READER,
YOU MAY WONDER WHY
AFTER ALL THESE CENTURIES
Santa Claus decided to write a book.
That is a good question.
You must understand
that I have my proper role in Christmas,
and I never felt it was my place to write about it.
Let others write about Christmas,
I always thought.
Charles Dickens, O. Henry, Truman Capote —
they wrote marvelous Christmas stories,
wonderful, wonderful stories.
I am not a writer, I always thought.
It is my place to be Santa Claus
and to participate in the Christmas festivities
as Santa is supposed to do.
That, I always felt,
is how things should be.

But in recent years something changed.
I try to stay in touch with the world
all year around, you know,
not just on Christmas.
Oh yes, I try to keep current
on current events,
and what I notice in recent years
is both an emptiness in the human heart
I never noticed before
and a longing for something more,
something deeper.
I believe that today, as never before,
there is a profound need for Christmas
and the spirit of Christmas.
I decided that maybe it would help
if Santa Claus himself wrote a small book
about Christmas
and about his memories and reflections
on Christmas and its deepest meaning.
If I try to remind people
about the true meaning of Christmas
perhaps that will help everyone
to not feel so empty;
perhaps that will help people to find
the "something more" they crave.
Perhaps people will listen to Santa Claus...

Because I am Santa Claus,
I remember every single person as a child.
I pay special attention to the children of the world
on Christmas, of course,
but when those children grow up
and become adults,
even though they sometimes forget about me,
or no longer believe I am real,
I never forget about them.
Never.
I remember every person's heart
as it was in childhood.
Dear reader and friend,
here is the truth:
each person has,
sometimes hidden deep within,
the heart he or she had as a child.
Your child's heart is the source
of your deepest and best feelings
about Christmas.
Your child's heart
is the source of all the best choices you ever made
or ever will make.
Your child's heart
is the source of all the best thoughts you ever had
or ever will have.

Because I remember every person as a child
I have hope for the human race
and for the earth.
Perhaps that is why only I, Santa Claus,
could write a book such as this one.
I have great hope,
and I want to remind you of your child's heart
so you can be hopeful and joyful too.
Come with me.
Take my hand,
and think of yourself again as a child.
Allow me to help you find again
the feelings about Christmas,
and about life and the world all year around,
that you had as a child.
There is much cause for hope
and much cause for joy.
Santa Claus says so,
and would Santa Claus tell a lie?
There is much reason to hope.
Take my hand.
Let me show you what I mean.
Let me touch your heart
with the spirit of Christmas.
Come.
The sleigh and the reindeer are waiting...

One

I Am Santa Claus

AM Santa Claus.
I am Santa Claus,
and my origins are mysterious,
especially to me.
This I know, that I would not exist
were it not for what happened
on a wondrous clear night,
under a wondrous bright star,
some two thousand years ago.
Were it not for the birth of a Boy Child
in a village called Bethlehem,
some two thousand years ago,
there would be no Christmas
…and so, there would be no Santa Claus.
The world would be a very different place
had that Child not been born,
and for sure there would be no Christmas.
I am Santa Claus,
and it is my joy and privilege

15

to encourage the spirit of Christmas.
It is my joy and honor
to nourish the magical meaning of Christmas
for all kinds of people.
I do it for those whose hearts tell them
that the Boy Child born on that night so long ago
was the Divine Mystery
come as a human being
to bring liberation, healing, and mercy
to a weary world.
You must understand that my message
echoes the message of that Child
born so long ago.
Like him I stand for love,
generosity,
unselfishness,
kindness,
courage, and life.
Like him, I want people to live together in peace.
Unlike him, I am not the message itself;
I am not the offspring of the Divine Mystery,
only his unworthy servant.
At the same time,
I carry the magic and wonder of Christmas
for those whose hearts incline them in other ways.
My deep and jolly laughter,

my very image,
has no purpose but to remind people of the magic,
wonder, mystery, and love
at the heart of the Christmas season.
It is my task to remind everyone
that Christmas is a time
to think more of others
than of yourself.
I am Santa Claus,
and that is my only purpose,
the one and only reason
I join you each year at Christmastime,
to remind you of this.
I am Santa Claus, and my origins are mysterious,
especially to me.
Oh yes, especially to me.
I was never a child, I had no childhood,
I have always been an old man
...but I have always had the heart of a child.
Each year during the Christmas season
it is my purpose to remind you
that you also have the heart of a child.
I don't succeed with all grownups, of course.
Many adults allow their hearts
to grow old and cold,
and so they foolishly declare that I do not exist.

For such people it is true that I do not exist,
but I do not think their lives are better for that.

I am Santa Claus, and my origins are mysterious,
especially to me.
I know that in the fourth century
— just yesterday, to be sure —
there was a kind and generous man
whose name was Nicholas.
He lived in Myra,
in the country known today as Turkey,
in Asia Minor.
Nicholas was a priest
who became the bishop of Myra,
a down-at-the-heels piece of countryside
if ever there was one.
The people were as poor
as the proverbial church mice,
and among them Nicholas was known
for his goodness and generosity.
Some say that Nicholas was born wealthy
and after his parents died he gave away
all his money and possessions to the poor.

Here is the most famous story about Nicholas.
A poor man had three daughters,
and he could see no way out of his poverty.
The man was so poor
that he had no money
to give to prospective husbands
as dowries for his daughters.
Hearing of this, on three separate occasions
Nicholas crept to the poor man's home by night,
while everyone was asleep,
and tossed a small bag of gold
through the window
so the three girls could marry.
Nicholas loved children dearly,
and on one occasion three children died.
It was so sad.
But through his prayers
Nicholas returned the children to their parents
alive and jumping up and down.
This is where we get the Christmas tradition
of giving gifts to children.
I'll bet you did not know that.
I am Santa Claus,
and if good Saint Nicholas never existed
I would not exist either.
Am I Nicholas with a different name?

Yes.

And no.

I, Santa Claus, am more than Nicholas
and less than Nicholas.

For I have other connections as well.

In the old, old times the Germanic peoples
had a god named Thor, the god of thunder.

During the long, cold, dark winters
the people thought of Thor,
and they burned a Yule log.

Thor rode on a chariot pulled by two goats,
and he named the goats Cracker and Gnasher.

Am I, Santa Claus,
merely a modern version of Thor?

No.

And yes.

I am Santa Claus, and my origins are mysterious,
especially to me.

Were it not for Nicholas I would not exist,
and were it not for Thor
I would not be who I am.

I am both, and I am neither.

I am less, and I am more.

I am Santa Claus, and my origins are mysterious.

Especially to me.

I am as true as the heart of a child,

and I am as real as the brightest star
that shines on Christmas Eve.

I am Santa Claus,
and it is my mission each Christmas season
to encourage the magic, the wonder,
and the love
only Christmas can bring.
In North America I am Santa Claus.
But I must tell you that I have other names
in other lands.
In England they call me Father Christmas,
in France I am *Père Noël*,
and in Germany *Weihnachtsmann*.
Whatever people in various countries call me
it is always me, one and the same,
here to nourish the spirit of Christmas
in the hearts of grownups and children alike.
In Sweden they call me *Jultomten*,
where I am an elfin character
who brings gifts to children on Christmas Eve,
and in Denmark and Norway
they call me *Julenissen*.

Different names, even different appearances,
but the same spirit and the same purpose —
to spread the joy and love
of the Christmas season.
Where did my name, Santa Claus, come from?
It is a delightful story.
You see,
the first Dutch settlers who came to America
were very fond of Saint Nicholas —
in their language, *Sinter Nicklaus,*
later shortened to *Sinter Klaus.*
They even had a picture of Saint Nicholas
painted on the front of the ship they sailed in.
After these people settled in their new country,
they maintained their traditional affection
for Nicholas
by telling their children
that on the eve of the Feast of Saint Nicholas,
December 6,
the good old bishop would visit their homes
and leave gifts.
As the years went by,
English settlers liked the tradition
about Saint Nicholas
so much that they adopted it for their own.
Good things have a way of catching on.

When English-speaking children said
"Sinter Klaus,"
in their excitement it sounded like "Santy Claus"
or "Santa Claus."
As time passed my name became Santa Claus
for everyone.
It's rather a charming story, don't you think?
It's like the little boy
who pronounced "spaghetti" as "scabetti,"
and before long his whole family said "scabetti"
just for the fun of it.

Is it true what they say about me?
They say that I live at the North Pole,
and I tell you this is true.
It is as true as Christmas.
But what is the North Pole?
I will tell you.
I live at the North Pole,
but do not search for me in the snow and ice
at the top of the earth.
I live in the North Pole of your heart,
the place in your heart

23

that is the coldest and most difficult to get to
most of the time.
During the Christmas season,
with a little help from me,
and a little effort on your part,
that coldest part of your heart warms up a bit
in the spirit of the season,
and I, Santa Claus,
return to the world once more
from the North Pole of your heart.
They say that I have a workshop filled with elves
who tinker together toys for girls and boys.
Santa has a question for you, a scholarly question.
Must facts
be scientifically and historically verifiable
in order to be true?
Must television news people
be able to videotape something
and put it on the evening news
in order for that something to be true?
Oh, people.
Truth is so much larger,
so much deeper than that!
Do I have a workshop filled with elves
at the North Pole?
Remember, the North Pole where I live

is in your heart,
and in that same cold place
a child's capacity for play and creativity
also dwells.
In the North Pole of your heart
there are powers of playfulness and creativity
you rarely allow to come out.
Call them elves if you wish.
Why not?
During the Christmas season I, Santa Claus,
whisper in the North Pole of your heart.
"Give the elves a chance
to make something wonderful for you,"
I whisper.
"Give the elves in the North Pole of your heart
a chance to play."
Many people listen to my whisperings, you know.
Oh, a great many.
Watch the people who ice skate
on the frozen pond in New York's Central Park
amid the brightly colored lights
and sparkling holiday decorations.
Watch families all over the country
who make a family adventure
out of going to a Christmas tree lot
to buy a Christmas tree.

Some go out into a forest
and cut a tree for themselves,
and that is an adventure for sure.

It is said that I have a big white beard
and wear a bright red suit with white trim
and a red hat to match.
Is this truly what I look like?
This is the easiest question so far.
The answer is yes.
Plain and simple, yes.
And no.
In modern times my image came first
from the great American writer
Washington Irving,
who described Saint Nicholas as a jolly, stout man
who wore a hat with a wide brim and baggy pants,
and smoked a long pipe.
Washington Irving said
that I rode over the treetops in a wagon
and filled children's stockings with presents.
The costume I wear now,
all red with white fur trim,

came from Thomas Nast,
a delightfully talented
nineteenth-century American illustrator
who had the heart of a child.
Before the mid-1800s, as Saint Nicholas,
I was a tall, thin, elegant gentleman
who dressed like a bishop,
with a miter on my head,
and I rode a wonderful white horse.
Oh, I was grand!
But what I wear is not the point.
How I look is not the point.
Here is the point.
I dress as I do, in a special way,
because I am an extraordinary character.
I do not dress as you do
because I do not live as you live.
My whole purpose is to remind people
to have hope,
to be kind,
to share,
and to rejoice in the gift of being alive.
The only reason I am here each Christmas season
is to remind people
to stop being so solemn all the time
and smile.

The Truth About Christmas

Were I to dress in an ordinary fashion
that would make my task more difficult.
The costume I wear makes my job easier,
it helps people to see that I am something special
and Christmas is something special.

It is said that I travel in a sleigh pulled by reindeer,
and both sleigh and reindeer fly.
Is this true?
Of course it is true,
and I cannot begin to tell you how much fun it is.
Oh, to speed through the starry, silent night skies
of late December, behind eight flying reindeer,
is an experience beyond telling.
It's cold, oh yes, it's icy cold.
But my heart is warm,
and the love and joy of the Christmas season
warm me from the inside out,
right to the tips of my fingers and toes.
It is true what Clement Clarke Moore wrote
in his famous poem, however:
my nose does get to be as red as a cherry!
There is no part of my story that is not true,

although much of it is true
as the heart judges what is true,
not as newspapers judge what is true.
There is no place I cannot travel
because I come and go
in a sleigh pulled by reindeer
who fly through the air at a remarkable speed.
What I say is as true as Christmas
and as real as the brightest star
on Christmas Eve.

Do I stop at each house on Christmas Eve,
in the night, after everyone is asleep,
and leave brightly wrapped presents
under the tree?
Have you ever known a Christmas
when this did not happen?
"Well," some cold-hearted grownup may say,
"I bought those gifts in stores,
and it is I who paid for them."
Whatever happened to your heart?
Where is the heart of a child you once had?
I, Santa Claus, would like to know.

The Truth About Christmas

Did I not say that I live in the North Pole
of your heart?
When your gift-buying and gift-giving
is a true expression of love, respect, or gratitude,
then it is I who lead you to buy and to give
from a heart that has thawed a bit,
a heart that is warmer than usual.
For I am the spirit and champion
of unselfish giving.
It is I who bring the gifts,
even if you or someone else pays for them.

I am Santa Claus,
and I am married to Mrs. Claus.
Sometimes today,
in this era of equality and fair dealing,
people want to know what Mrs. Claus's name is.
Does she not have
an individual identity of her own,
apart from her relationship with me?
Well, you know,
we are rather an old-fashioned couple,
and Mrs. Claus is content to be called Mrs. Claus.

But if you must know, her name is Emma.
Emma Claus.
Before we married she was Emma Snoof.
Perhaps you can understand why she was happy
to change her name to mine.
Mrs. Claus considers it rude
if people address her by her first name.
She prefers to be called Mrs. Claus,
and if you ever meet her,
and want some of her home-baked sugar cookies,
you had better call not call her Emma.
"I am not a woman to be trifled with,"
Mrs. Claus often says,
and you had better believe her.

I am Santa Claus,
but sometimes parents worry
over whether they should tell their children
about me.
These are "enlightened" parents, of course,
"modern" parents
who do not want to tell their children
stories that are not true

as newspapers judge what is true.
Such parents no longer
have the heart of a child.
It is so exasperating.
I, Santa Claus, come to add to the mystery,
delight, and love
at the heart of the Christmas season.
It has always been my experience
that children who believe in me
do not receive permanent emotional
or psychological scars.
On the contrary!
Children whose parents tell them about me
often have a deeper inclination to wonder and joy
all their lives long.
They are more likely to become Christmas people,
people who each year embrace Christmas
and celebrate it with all their heart.
Put yourself in my place.
How would you like it
if parents told their children
that you do not exist?
Honestly.
I am Santa Claus, and my origins are mysterious,
especially to me.
This I know, that I am as old as the stars

and as young as Christmas Eve.
I will always be an old man
with a long white beard,
and I will always live at the North Pole.
I will always make a list
and check it twice.
My reindeer will always pull my sleigh
through the night skies on Christmas Eve
to leave toys and candy for children
and for grownups
who still have the heart of a child.
I am Santa Claus, and I am forever.
This I know.
Do you still have your doubts?
Hush.
Listen to your heart.
Come closer, let me whisper in your ear.
Merry Christmas! Ho! Ho! Ho!

Two

I Remember

CHRISTMASTIME IS A TIME
OF MYSTERY AND WONDER,
A TIME OF MEMORIES UPON MEMORIES.
If Christmas is anything, it is memories
that come alive here and now.
I am Santa Claus, and this I know.
Each Christmas we recall earlier Christmases,
and each Christmas
we build more Christmas memories
to cherish in later years.
Christmas has a special power
to touch the heart;
it has a special power to touch the heart
because it is a time for nostalgia.
Nostalgia? What's this? Nostalgia?
People think that nostalgia is nothing
but a sentimental longing for the past,
and sometimes that is true.
But there can be more to nostalgia than that.

37

Much more. Listen.
Sometimes I, Santa Claus, like to play the scholar.
So listen.
I stand at the front of the classroom,
forefinger raised in the air.
Ahem.
One of the roots of the word "nostalgia"
is the Old English,
Old High German,
and Old Norse word
nest,
which means "food for a journey."
Can you imagine that?
It is also related to the Greek word
nostos,
which means "a return home."
So listen.
This is what I mean
when I use the word "nostalgia."
I mean memories
as a source of vitality and strength,
and memories as a way
to turn toward our heart's true home.
Yes.
In our Christmas memories
we find strength to deal with the present,

and we find the hope and courage we need
to build the future.
In our Christmas memories
we rediscover our longing
for our heart's true home,
and this helps us to find our true home
here and now.
My name is Santa Claus, not Pollyanna.
Some Christmas memories are sad memories.
But even a sad Christmas memory
can be a source of strength
and a guiding light.
To remember a sad Christmas from the past
can help us to appreciate more
the Christmas we have right now.
It can help us to help others
have a happy Christmas this year.
You have your treasury of nourishing nostalgia,
and I have mine.
I am Santa Claus,
and I would share some of my nostalgia,
my Christmas memories,
with you.
Listen closely, now.
Listen with an open heart.
Listen...

Clement Clarke Moore's
Christmas Poem

Part the curtains of the past.
Part the curtains of the past and look back.
Look back to the second decade
of the nineteenth century.
Here is perhaps my fondest Christmas memory.
Look and you will see an old friend of mine,
a man who understood me
as no one understood me before or since.
The man's name is Clement Clarke Moore,
and he is a minister, poet, and professor
at a seminary in New York City.
Clement is a scholar of the Bible,
so it makes sense that he would understand
the spirit of Christmas.
It makes sense
that he would understand Santa Claus too.
In fact,
Clem never called me Santa Claus,
no, not ever at all.
He always called me Saint Nicholas.
Look.
It is some days before Christmas
in the astonishing year of 1822.

New York City is downright pastoral,
not a skyscraper in sight.
Central Park, such as it is, is like a pasture.
No one has even thought
of St. Patrick's Cathedral,
which will become the tallest structure in the city.
Construction will begin
some thirty years in the future,
and the cathedral won't be completed
for more than fifty years, in 1879.
Clement Moore sits at his desk, writing,
an oil lamp casts its flickering light
as his pen scratches away.
Clem works on a poem for his children,
a poem he thought about all day,
a poem that will be
their most special Christmas present this year.
Filled with the joy of the Christmas season,
Clem Moore asks himself about Saint Nicholas,
for this is who Santa Claus
gets much of his spirit from,
and before long Clem's heart tells him
what to write.
He dips his pen in his ink pot,
scratches words on paper,
and when he is done he has what will become

the most famous poem and story
about Saint Nicholas,
and Santa Claus,
ever written.
He calls his poem
"A Visit from St. Nicholas."

That Christmas of 1822
Clement Moore gave his poem to his children;
he read it to them for Christmas.
They were delighted.
The children laughed, and clapped,
and jumped up and down.
They asked their father to read the poem
over and over,
and he did so with tears in his eyes
so great was the joy he knew,
so deep was the joy he saw in his children's eyes.
Clement Moore was a happy man.
The next year, 1823,
a relative of Clement Moore
gave a copy of his poem
to a friend,

who showed it to the editor of a newspaper,
the *Troy Sentinel*.
The editor was so impressed
that a couple of days before Christmas,
he published Clement Moore's poem.
But Clem was so modest
that his name did not appear with the poem.
For quite a long time people did not know
that he had written this wonderful poem.
But I knew.
Years later, some people claimed
that the poem was written by a land surveyor
named Henry Livingston, Jr.
Now Henry was a fine fellow,
and he wrote some poems too.
But I know that Clement Moore wrote the poem
that came to be known as
"'Twas the Night Before Christmas."
I am Santa Claus, and I know.
Because I was there...
Here is Clem Moore's Christmas present
to his children,
the poem that has come to be called
"'Twas the Night Before Christmas."
Read it slowly; let it rest in your heart.
If possible, read it slowly with a child on your lap.

The Truth About Christmas

If you cannot find a child to put on your lap,
then read this good, gentle, happy poem
with the heart of a child yourself...

'Twas the Night Before Christmas
by Clement Clarke Moore

'Twas the night before Christmas,
when all through the house
not a creature was stirring, not even a mouse.
The stockings were hung
by the chimney with care,
in hopes that St. Nicholas soon would be there.
The children were nestled all snug in their beds,
while visions of sugar plums
danced in their heads.
And Mama in her kerchief, and I in my cap,
had just settled our brains for a long winter's nap.
When out on the roof there arose such a clatter,
I sprang from my bed to see what was the matter.
Away to the windows I flew like a flash,
tore open the shutter, and threw up the sash.
The moon on the breast of the new-fallen snow
gave the lustre of midday to objects below,
when, what to my wondering eyes should appear,
but a miniature sleigh and eight tiny reindeer.

With a little old driver, so lively and quick,
I knew in a moment it must be St. Nick.
More rapid than eagles, his coursers they came,
and he whistled and shouted
and called them by name:

"Now Dasher! Now Dancer!
Now, Prancer and Vixen!
On, Comet! On Cupid!
On, Donner and Blitzen!
To the top of the porch! To the top of the wall!
Now dash away! Dash away! Dash away all!"

As dry leaves that before the wild hurricane fly,
when they meet with an obstacle,
mount to the sky,
so up to the house-top the coursers they flew,
with the sleigh full of toys, and St. Nicholas too.
And then, in a twinkling, I heard on the roof
the prancing and pawing of each little hoof.
As I drew in my head and was turning around,
down the chimney St. Nicholas
came with a bound.

He was dressed all in fur,
from his head to his foot,

and his clothes were all tarnished
with ashes and soot.
A bundle of toys he had flung on his back,
and he looked like a peddler just opening his pack.
His eyes — how they twinkled!
His dimples, how merry!
His cheeks were like roses, his nose like a cherry!
His droll little mouth was drawn up like a bow,
and the beard of his chin
was as white as the snow.

The stump of a pipe he held tight in his teeth,
and the smoke, it encircled his head like a wreath.
He had a broad face and a little round belly,
that shook when he laughed,
like a bowl full of jelly.
He was chubby and plump, a right jolly old elf,
and I laughed when I saw him, in spite of myself.
A wink of his eye and a twist of his head
soon gave me to know I had nothing to dread.

He spoke not a word,
but went straight to his work,
and filled all the stockings,
then turned with a jerk.
And laying his finger aside of his nose,

and giving a nod, up the chimney he rose.
He sprang to his sleigh, to his team gave a whistle,
and away they all flew like the down of a thistle.
But I heard him exclaim,
ere they drove out of sight,
"Happy Christmas to all, and to all a good night!"

One of the Best Pictures
of Santa Claus Ever

I want to tell you
about the picture of me on the cover of this book.
As you probably already know,
it was painted by the great American artist
Norman Rockwell.
I believe it may be the best portrait of me
done by anyone, anyplace, ever,
because it captures me as Santa Claus
while the halo above my head
reminds people that in my heart
I am Saint Nicholas.
the boy balanced on my fingers
reminds everyone of my love for children
and my quest for the spirit of childhood
in everyone.
Norman Rockwell drew or painted

many pictures of me
over the years,
but all except this one
he did from his imagination.
This one he did from his heart,
and this one I posed for in person.
Here is how it happened.
In 1927
the editors of *The Saturday Evening Post*,
in Philadelphia, Pennsylvania,
wanted a picture of Santa Claus
for the cover of the December issue
of their magazine.
Norman Rockwell did a rough sketch
and sent it to the editors.
They gave him the go-ahead
to do the final illustration.

Norman Rockwell wanted this to be
a very special picture of Santa Claus.
So he called on me.
Norman Rockwell was thirty-three years old
in 1927,
and he called on me
in the North Pole of his heart.
Just after New Year's Day, in 1927,

Norman Rockwell asked me to pose for a portrait.
No one had ever asked me to pose before,
so I was as surprised as could be.
But I agreed.
I admired Norman Rockwell's work,
and I knew he had a wonderful future
ahead of him,
even though he wasn't as famous in 1927
as he would one day become.
So I agreed to "sit" for him.
In June of 1927,
I visited Norman Rockwell's studio
on Lord Kichener Road,
in New Rochelle, New York,
and "sat" for him while he painted.
It was very warm for June,
so Norman Rockwell decided
to paint just my face.
Below my neck,
as Norman Rockwell painted me,
I was wearing a tee-shirt, cut-offs, and sandals!
Still, it was a hot day, and
that's why my face is so red in the picture.
A red face can as easily come from the cold,
of course,
which is why it looks appropriate in the picture.

I stayed with Norman Rockwell
for three days.
No one else in New Rochelle recognized me.
People thought I was just someone
from out of town
whom Norman Rockwell had asked
to pose for him.
Since this was an exception to my rule
that I never leave the North Pole
except at Christmastime,
I made Norman Rockwell promise
he would tell no one
about my visit to his studio
on Lord Kichener Road.
He kept his promise.
Not even the people at *The Saturday Evening Post*
know that the portrait they published
was a life portrait of Santa Claus.
But now *you* know.

Teresa's Christmas Eve

I, Santa Claus, am a busy man,
especially on Christmas Eve.
My work must be done all in one night.
Most people do not need to work

on Christmas Eve, of course.
Christmas Eve is a time to be home,
to be with family and friends,
and for many it is a time
to join a community of worship.
But I, Santa Claus, am aware
that this beautiful ideal
is not part of everyone's experience.
More good people than you might imagine
have a Christmas Eve
you would not want for yourself.
I remember one Christmas Eve,
not so many years ago.
The night sky was cold and clear,
the stars as bright as could be.
I recall a woman
whose family I had visited many times.
Teresa, her name was. Teresa.
She lived near a farming community,
her house rather isolated
and easy to identify as I flew over.
I was startled to see that the house was dark.
No cheerful fire,
no excited grandchildren
finding it difficult to get to sleep
on Christmas Eve.

Then I realized where Teresa was.
I have a sixth sense, you know,
an instinct which enables me
to locate people from one Christmas to the next.
Teresa lived now in a convalescent home,
her health failing,
where people worked who could take care of her.
I decided to peek in on Teresa
to see the kind of Christmas Eve
she would have that year.
The windows of the home were frosty,
but I could see Teresa
sitting in a large room
with many other men and women
of her own generation.
She did not look happy.
Teresa sat in a wheelchair,
an old sweater over her shoulders.
A television set flickered
in one corner of the room.
Someone had tried to decorate the room
for Christmas,
but the attempt was not entirely successful.
I was sorry to see Teresa in this situation.
This was not the kind of Christmas Eve
she had for so many years.

I wondered where her adult children were,
her grandchildren and great-grandchildren.
Why did they not come
and take her to one of their homes
for Christmas Eve?
Did they all live too far away?
I wish I could tell you that as I watched,
in through the door came
a crowd of merry relatives
to whisk Teresa away
to jolly Christmas Eve festivities
someplace else.
But I cannot tell you that.
It was time for me to move on,
and as far as I know
Teresa spent her entire Christmas
right there in that convalescent home.
I hope not, but I wouldn't be surprised.
Many, many older people
have little joy on Christmas, you know.
I, Santa Claus, would appreciate it
if you would make some small effort
to bring Christmas joy
into the lives of some older people
who no longer live in their own homes.
It is trite to say so,

but it is so true, as well.
The more you give joy
the more joy you will receive.
Think.
Think of people who are homeless.
Think of people who are hungry.
On Christmas Eve remember people
who are hungry and have no home,
people who are old and lonely.
Do something for them,
and you will begin to understand
the true meaning of Christmas
and the true meaning of Santa Claus.

Dr. Seuss, the Grinch, and I

One of my favorite memories of Christmas
happened in the middle of May!
Sometimes people begin planning for Christmas
in advance,
and this was one of those times.
Just about everyone knows about Dr. Seuss
and his famous story,
How the Grinch Stole Christmas!
Dr. Seuss had a wild and wonderful imagination.
What a friend of mine he was.

Dr. Seuss's real name was Theodore Geisel,
you know
— his friends called him Ted —
but in his heart he was Dr. Seuss,
and he dreamed up wonderful characters
for all his stories,
and this one was no exception.
You remember the Grinch, of course,
and the Whos who live in Whoville,
and the Grinch's dog, Max.
Not many people know, however,
that I had something to do
with the writing of this particular book.
This is one of my most delightful
Christmas memories,
and it happened not in December but May.
Dr. Seuss lived in California for many years,
and in 1957 he decided to write
a Christmas story,
but he could not think of a story idea.
He wracked his brain,
but he could not come up with an idea
for a Christmas story.
He wanted to remind people
of the spiritual meaning of Christmas,
but that was all he knew.

Dr. Seuss loved Christmas,
but he puzzled and puzzled,
and no idea would come.
He was very frustrated.
Then he realized that what he needed
was a story about
the deepest meaning of Christmas
told in a way simple enough
for even grownups to understand.
Dr. Seuss had no doubt
that most children understood Christmas;
it was grownups he was worried about,
plus the occasional child
who thinks that Christmas
is about stockpiling loot.
Early in the month of May
Dr. Seuss wrote me a letter.
He kept it a secret, of course,
since no one writes letters to Santa in May.
He told no one,
not even his wife, Helen,
and most certainly not his publisher,
Bennett Cerf.
Dr. Seuss wrote a letter to me.
I still have it in my files,
and here it is:

May 9, 1957

Dear Santa Claus,

I am having a hard time trying to think of a Christmas story to write. People — sometimes even children — are forgetting the true Christmas spirit. They think Christmas is all about buying stuff. I want to write a story so simple that children, and even grownups, can understand it. Do you have any ideas? I will appreciate any help you can offer.

Your friend,
Ted Geisel (Dr. Seuss)

You can imagine my surprise
when I received this letter
from the famous Dr. Seuss.
Very often the younger elves
ask me to read a story at bedtime,
and very often they ask for a Dr. Seuss story.
They are especially fond
of *Green Eggs and Ham,*
as well as Dr. Seuss's very first book,
And to Think That It Happened on Mulberry Street.
Another favorite of the elves is
The 500 Hats of Bartholomew Cubbins.
I was astonished and delighted

when I saw who the letter was from.
I was surprised to receive a letter
from anybody in May,
but I was even more surprised
to see that this letter
was from the wonderful Dr. Seuss.
"Imagine," I thought.
"Dr. Seuss wrote to *me*,
one of his biggest fans,
and he wants me to suggest
an idea for a Christmas story."
The elves were impressed, I can tell you!
I thought and thought for many days.
What kind of story could Dr. Seuss write
for Christmas?
He wanted to write a story
that looked like it was for children
but was really for adults
and children who lose sight
of the true meaning of Christmas.
This was no easy assignment...
I thought and thought.
I asked Mrs. Claus to think.
I asked the reindeer and the elves to think.
So everyone thought.
We wracked our brains.

There are so many people
who think Christmas is presents
and lights
and decorated trees.
So many people think
that Christmas
is a big Christmas dinner.
So many people forget
that Christmas is above all
a spirit of love,
generosity, and kindness,
a spirit that has no real need
for presents,
lights,
decorated trees,
and big Christmas dinners,
nice as all these things are, of course.
I began to wonder if Dr. Seuss
could write a story that would get this idea across.
Perhaps he could think up a mean character
who would try to deprive people of Christmas
by taking away all the trappings of Christmas,
only to discover that Christmas
requires none of the trappings at all.
Here is the letter I wrote back to Dr. Seuss,
I still have a copy in my files:

May 15, 1957

Dear Ted,

I was most flattered to receive your letter, as I am a big fan, and the younger elves often ask me to read your books aloud at bedtime. I agree that many people, young and old, frequently forget the true meaning of Christmas. I hope you will be able to write a story that will help.

I have thought about it, and the only idea I came up with would go something like this: A mean character — perhaps you could name him "Flinch" or "Grouchpile," or something like that — is so mean-spirited that he despises Christmas with all its joy. All this could happen in Walla Walla, Washington, which is a funny name for a town, don't you think? You could have Grouchpile, or whatever you name him, live in a cave in the side of a mountain outside of town. He could have a cat named Rat Face. Grouchpile could have an old car, drive into town on Christmas Eve, and steal all the Christmas trees in Walla Walla, thinking this would make people so angry they would forget to have Christmas.

But in the end, even though Grouchpile took all the Christmas trees, the people in Walla Walla would have Christmas all the same. At first they would get angry, but then they would be reminded of the spirit of Christmas by a little girl — you could name her Mary — and they would get over being angry about the stolen Christmas trees. I hope this is some help.

Your friend,
Santa Claus

As you can see,
Dr. Seuss wrote a much better story
than the one I suggested,
which was pretty bad.
All the same,
my letter did get the wheels turning
in Dr. Seuss's head,
and he wrote a marvelous Christmas story
loved by countless children
and grownups as well.
I always get a kick out of the fact
that Dr. Seuss had the Grinch
try to impersonate me.
The Grinch wears
the silliest Santa Claus costume ever!
I love it!

The True Believer

Nothing warms my heart like a grownup,
especially an older person,
who truly believes in me.
One afternoon many years ago,
a man named Joe,
who did an outstanding job of impersonating me
was on duty in a department store.
Joe was a big man
who filled his Santa costume well,
and he had a wonderful, jolly laugh.
Everyone said that he made a grand Santa Claus.
Joe sat in his special chair
and took children on his lap
to listen to what they would like for Christmas.
This particular day,
Joe noticed an elderly lady
who watched him for a long time
as he visited with children of all ages.
The little old lady stayed around
all afternoon,
even when daylight began to fade
and the shoppers began leaving for home.
The lady watched Joe,
a sad, wistful look on her face.

Finally, all the children were gone
and Joe prepared to leave for the day.
He glanced up,
and there stood the little old lady
who had been watching him all afternoon.
In the lady's eyes Jim recognized something,
something he rarely saw,
even in the eyes of children.
Joe saw that this lady
truly believed in Santa Claus,
and she truly believed that *he* was Santa Claus —
which, in a very real way, he was,
so successfully did he make my spirit present.
Joe left his chair
and walked over to where the lady stood.
As Joe approached the old lady
the expression on her face changed
from one of sad wistfulness
to an expression of innocent joy.
The old lady's face became
the face of a child.
Drawing near,
Joe held out his arms to the old lady.
"It's so good to see you!" he exclaimed,
his voice filled with delight.
The old lady's eyes filled with tears of joy.

"Yes, Santa," the old lady replied.
"I've been waiting for you all afternoon."
Joe gathered the old lady into his arms,
the arms of Santa Claus,
and gave her a wonderful hug.
Joe and the old lady talked for a long time.
They talked about the old lady's childhood,
about where she had grown up,
about her brothers and sisters,
and about her grandchildren.
Finally, Joe gave the lady another hug,
she thanked him for visiting with her,
and she walked away,
out of the store.
Behind her the old lady left more Christmas
than had been there before.

St. Francis of Assisi and the Manger Scene

As Santa Claus
my purpose is to make present
the true spirit of Christmas
and remind people of the deepest meaning
of Christmas.
As I said earlier in this book,

even though Christmas means many things
to many people
there would have been no Christmas
in the first place
were it not for the birth of a Boy Child
in Bethlehem
some two thousand years ago.
Another of my favorite Christmas memories
concerns a man who lived in Italy
from the late twelfth
to the early thirteenth centuries.
His name was Francis Bernadone,
and he was a devoted follower
of the man that Boy Child became.
Today most people know Francis Bernadone
as Saint Francis of Assisi.
People for whom Christmas
is mainly a celebration
of the birth of the Child of Bethlehem
often place in their homes and churches
manger scenes representing
the birth of that Child.
Many people do not realize, however,
that Saint Francis of Assisi
was the first one to do this
more than five hundred years ago...

About two weeks before Christmas,
in the year 1223,
Brother Francis wanted to celebrate the birth
of "the Babe of Bethlehem"
—which is what Francis called him—
in a special way.
Being in the little town of Greccio at the time,
Francis called for a knight by the name of John
who lived there
and was a great friend of Francis.
When John arrived,
Francis greeted him warmly.
Francis said that this Christmas
he wanted to do something special
to remind people of the little Child
who was born in Bethlehem.
He told John that he wanted to reconstruct
in some manner
the scene in which the Child was born
to show in what poverty,
simplicity, and humility
he came into the world,
how he lay upon a bed of hay in a manger

with an ox and a donkey standing nearby.
John, hearing what Francis wanted
and anxious to be of service,
hurried off
and began to prepare the manger scene
exactly as Francis requested.
It was not difficult to find an ox and a donkey,
for such animals
were common in those days.
John prepared a place
where the animals stood near a manger,
or feedbox,
and he filled it with straw.
In later times
people would add the figures
of Mary, Joseph, and the Child
to the scene,
as well as the Magi,
but this first time there would be only the animals
and the empty manger filled with straw.
On Christmas Eve,
all the people from Greccio
and the surrounding countryside,
and all of Francis's followers
came to celebrate Christmas
at the manger scene.

The forest around Greccio
echoed with their songs,
the music resounded from the very rocks,
and the night was lit up with many bright lights
from burning torches.
Brother Francis stood before the manger,
and his heart was filled with joy.
With a priest presiding,
Francis and all the people
sang a beautiful Christmas Mass,
and Francis, who was a deacon,
sang the story of the birth of the Child
from the scriptures.
Then he preached to the people
about the birth of the poor King,
whom he called the Babe of Bethlehem.
Francis encouraged the people
to love little things and simple things.
Later, Francis's friend John
said that as Francis preached
the Child appeared, lying in the manger,
and Francis tenderly took him in his arms,
and the sleeping Child awoke.
I do not doubt it for a second.
After the celebration was over
the people took straws from the manger

as souvenirs,
and they said later
that when they fed the straw to sick animals
the animals were cured.
Imagine that...

A Christmas for Della and Jim

After Clement Moore's
"'Twas the Night Before Christmas,"
my favorite Christmas story
was written by a man who went by the name
of O. Henry,
who lived from 1862 to 1910.
Actually, his name was William Sydney Porter,
but he thought it was fun
when he wrote stories
to use the name O. Henry.
So that is what everyone calls him
to this day.
O. Henry was a great writer,
but he didn't make much money from his writing.
So he had to take other jobs,
and one time one of those other jobs
got him into big trouble.
He worked for a bank,

and he wasn't very good at math.
He was so bad at adding and subtracting
that he made some mistakes,
and it looked like he had stolen some money
from the bank.
Frightened, O. Henry made yet another mistake
by running away.
He went all the way to Honduras,
a country in South America.
O. Henry didn't realize
that he would be pardoned
because he did not really steal any money
from the bank.
In 1896,
O. Henry returned to the United States
because his wife, who had stayed behind,
was very sick.
The police arrested him
and put him in prison for three years.
Even in prison, however,
O. Henry wrote stories under various names.
O. Henry wrote a great many stories.
In fact, he had about fourteen volumes of stories
published in his lifetime.
But his most famous story is called
"The Gift of the Magi,"

and I think it a great story
about the true meaning of Christmas.
I hope you will read the original story yourself,
but for now I would like to tell you the story
in my own words.
Listen, now.
There is so much love and Christmas joy
in this story:

It was the mid-1800s, in New York City,
and a young woman named Della
counted her money.
One dollar and eighty-seven cents,
that was all,
and sixty cents was in pennies
she had saved by bargaining with the butcher,
the grocer, and the vegetable man.
Della counted her money three times
to make sure her count was correct.
One dollar and eighty-seven cents,
and tomorrow would be Christmas.
Della saw that there was nothing to do
but throw herself down
on the threadbare little couch
and cry.
So that is what she did.

After she finished crying,
Della dried her tears,
took a deep breath,
and attended to her burning cheeks
with a powder puff.
Then she stood by the apartment window
and looked out at a drab gray cat
walking along a drab gray fence
in a drab gray backyard.
Della had only one dollar and eighty-seven cents
to buy her husband, Jim,
a Christmas present.
She must find something fine and wonderful,
something worthy of James Dillingham Young.
Something worthy of *her Jim.*
Suddenly, Della turned from the window
and stood before the mirror.
Quickly, she undid her hair
and let it cascade down her back
to its full length.
There were two possessions
Della and Jim were extremely proud of.
One was Jim's gold pocket watch,
which had belonged to his father
and to his grandfather.
The other was Della's gorgeous hair.

If a queen had lived next door,
Della's hair would have put to shame
Her Majesty's royal jewels.
If Solomon had been the janitor
in the apartment building,
with all his wealth piled up in the basement,
he would have envied Jim
his gold pocket watch.
Her hands shaking,
Della put up her beautiful hair.
She donned her old brown winter coat
and her old brown hat.
For just a moment she paused,
as a tear rolled down her cheek
and onto the worn red carpet.
Then Della took control of herself,
opened the door,
and was out in the street
before she could reflect anymore
on what she planned to do.
Della walked as fast as she could,
and when she stopped,
she stood before a little shop,
and in the window there was a sign:
"Mme. Sofronie, Hair Goods Bought and Sold.
All Kinds."

Della ran up one flight of stairs,
and still breathing heavily
she asked Mme. Sofronie,
"Will you buy my hair?"
"I do buy hair," the woman nodded.
"Remove your hat, please,
and let me take a look at it."
Della undid her hair
for the second time that morning,
and down it fell,
the richest, most luxurious hair Mme. Sofronie
had seen in years.
"I will give you twenty dollars,"
Mme. Sofronie said.
Now in the mid-1800s
twenty dollars was a lot of money,
so Mme. Sofronie's price was more than fair.
"That will be fine," Della said.
"Please, hurry,
take my hair and give me the money."
The next two hours flew by in a haze of joy
as Della hurried from one store to the next
looking for a Christmas present for Jim.
At last, she found the perfect gift.
Jim would no longer need to use
a worn old leather strap

for the gold pocket watch he had inherited
from his father and his grandfather.
For Christmas this year
Della would give him a platinum watch chain,
simple yet elegant in design,
a watch chain worthy
of Jim's gold pocket watch.
Twenty-one dollars was the price,
and Della hurried back with what she had left,
eighty-seven cents.
Home once again,
Della used her curling irons
to cover her head with curls
so she bore an astonishing resemblance
to a mischievous schoolboy.
Then, she waited.
Jim would be home before long.
When she heard Jim's step on the staircase
she stopped breathing
for just a moment.
Della was in the habit
of saying simple little prayers,
at odd times,
about the simple things of everyday life.
She whispered, "Dear God,
please help Jim to think I am still pretty."

The door opened.
Jim came in,
but instead of his usual smile
he looked cold and serious.
The poor guy was only twenty-two years old,
after all,
and he badly needed a new coat
and had no gloves.
The second Jim saw Della
his face took on an expression
that almost frightened her.
He was neither angry nor surprised.
He did not seem to disapprove
of what he saw,
and he was not horrified.
Della might have expected any of these reactions.
Instead, Jim stared at Della
with the strangest look on his face.
Della ran into Jim's arms.
"Jim, my love, don't be upset with me.
I had my hair cut off and sold it
because I couldn't bear the thought of Christmas
with no gift for you.
My hair grows awfully fast, you know,
and it will grow out again.
You won't mind, will you?

Say 'Merry Christmas!' Jim,
and let's be happy."
"You cut off your hair?"
Jim said with an effort.
"Yes. I cut it off and sold it.
You'll like me just as much
without my long hair,
won't you, Jim?"
Jim looked around the room,
his eyes rather vacant.
Then he began to grin
almost idiotically.
"Your hair is gone?" he asked.
"Please try to understand," Della pleaded.
"It's Christmas Eve!
My hair isn't that important,
and it *will* grow back.
What matters is that I love you,
and nothing can ever change that."
Jim seemed to snap out
of some kind of trance.
He took Della into his arms again
and hugged her.
Then from the pocket of his thin coat
he took a small package
and tossed it on the table.

"Don't get me wrong," Jim said.
"Cutting your hair off
could never change my love for you.
But if you will unwrap that package,
you will see why you had me mystified
for a minute there."
Della tore open the package,
tossing bits of paper and string
every which way.
She let out a scream of joy
which quickly changed to crying and tears.
It took all Jim could do
to calm her down.
For there on the table
lay the beautiful set of combs
Della had admired for many months
in a store window not far away.
The combs were beautiful and expensive,
pure tortoiseshell with jewels on the rims,
combs to wear in her beautiful hair
that now was no more.
Even knowing she could never have the combs,
Della had yearned for them all the same.
Now the combs belonged to her,
but the hair they should have adorned
was gone.

All the same,
Della picked up the combs
and hugged them to herself.
Through her tears she said,
"Oh, Jim, my hair grows fast!"
Then Della remembered
her present for Jim.
"Oh, oh!" she exclaimed.
She held out to Jim a package
with her present for him inside.
Slowly he opened the small box,
and inside the precious metal seemed to glow
with something of Della's own loving spirit.
"Isn't it dandy, Jim?
I looked all over town for it.
Now you'll have to check the time
a hundred times a day.
Give me your watch
so I can see how it looks on it."
Instead of doing as he was told,
Jim collapsed on the couch,
his hands behind his head,
a big smile on his face.
"Dell," he said,
"let's put our Christmas presents away for a while.
I sold my watch so I could buy your combs."

I, Santa Claus,
love this story
because it carries the true meaning
of Christmas.
This story carries the mystery.
So goes the story of a young husband and wife
who knew the real meaning of love
and the real meaning of Christmas gift-giving.
They knew that a gift means little
unless it costs more than money.
Do you wonder how to give gifts at Christmas?
Pay attention to the story of Della and Jim.
They each sacrificed something they loved
in order to give something to the other.
If all our Christmas gifts cost us
is money
then we don't fully grasp
the meaning of Christmas.
That is the mystery,
and that is the joy of Christmas.

Good King Wenceslas

One of my favorite Christmas carols
is "Good King Wenceslas."
You remember how it starts:

> *Good King Wenceslas looked out*
> *On the feast of Stephen,*
> *When the snow lay round about,*
> *Deep and crisp and even...*

The song goes on to tell
how Wenceslas and his page
faced the "winter's rage"
to take food, wine, and firewood
to a poor peasant.
In the song Good King Wenceslas
shows that he understands
the true meaning of Christmas.
The story the old carol tells
is probably just a story.
As is often the case
with Christmas stories, however,
this old carol rings with
the true message of Christmas.
The song is just a song,

but Wenceslas was a real person,
and he understood Christmas.
Here is the true story
of the actual Good King Wenceslas.

Wenceslas lived in Bohemia,
in what is now Czechoslovakia,
a long time ago,
some thousand years ago, in fact.
His father was a duke named Ratislav,
and his mother, Drahomira,
was the daughter of a tribal chieftain.
Wenceslas had a younger brother,
Boleslas.
Wenceslas's parents had no interest
in goodness and kindness,
but he was raised by his pious grandmother,
Ludmila.
Boleslas, on the other hand,
grew up with his parents,
and later on it would show.
About the year 920,
Wenceslas's father died in battle.

His mother, Drahomira,
no slouch at politics herself,
took control of the government.
Under the influence
of certain evil nobles, however,
she became a cruel ruler
who was unjust and unkind.
This displeased the good Ludmila,
who explained to her grandson, Wenceslas,
that he must take control of the government
in order to restore justice and peace.
The evil nobles who backed Drahomira
learned what Wenceslas and his grandmother
were up to,
and two of these uncouth cads,
figuring that if they got rid of the grandmother
the grandson would beat a hasty retreat,
went to Ludmila and strangled her to death.
Unfortunately for the evil nobles, however,
in 922 men opposed to Drahomira banished her
and proclaimed Wenceslas the new king.
The young ruler announced
that he would promote justice and kindness,
punish murderers severely,
and strive to rule all his subjects
with compassion.

To prove how compassionate he would be,
Wenceslas recalled his mother from exile.
When Wenceslas's wife bore him a son,
about the year 926,
Boleslas, the younger brother,
was enraged.
This meant that he was no longer
a successor to the throne,
so in true spoil-sport fashion
Boleslas joined the disloyal opposition.
He then did Wenceslas the darkest of deeds.
On September 20, 926,
the pious Wenceslas was on his way to church.
In front of the chapel
he met his brother, Boleslas,
and greeted him kindly.
Boleslas responded by hitting Wenceslas
upside the head,
and the two brothers fell to the ground struggling.
A group of Boleslas's friends ran up
and killed Wenceslas,
who murmured as he fell against the chapel door,
"Brother, may God forgive you."
As such things sometimes went in those days,
before long the people proclaimed
Good King Wenceslas

a martyr for the faith,
even though his death
had more to do with politics
than religion.
By the end of the tenth century
Wenceslas became the patron saint
of the Bohemian people,
and today he is the official patron saint
of Czechoslovakia.
All very interesting,
but how did Wenceslas
end up in an English Christmas carol?
The words of "Good King Wenceslas"
were written by
the nineteenth-century hymn writer
J. M. Neal
to fit a thirteenth-century tune.
It's as simple as that.
Even if the story in the carol is legendary,
it carries the spirit of Good King Wenceslas,
the spirit of kindness,
generosity,
and justice,
and that is what Christmas is about.

Santa Claus Impersonators

Every Christmas season,
I, Santa Claus,
manage to be in thousands of places
at the same time,
but it's not much of a mystery.
All across the countryside, men
— and sometimes women — dress up like me.
It's quite a tribute, actually.
I am so popular
that people dress up like me
in order to make the spirit of Santa Claus
and the spirit of Christmas
more present
and remind people
of the true meaning of Christmas.
I, Santa Claus, love it.
True, sometimes the Santa Claus costumes
that people put on
are a bit phony looking,
but I guess they cannot help that.
Their intention is good,
and their hearts are in the right place.
Some of my warmest Christmas memories
are of Santa Claus impersonators.

These people bring so much joy,
especially to children,
every Christmas season,
that I love them dearly.
It is especially thrilling to me
when Santa impersonators
go to visit children
who must be in a hospital at Christmastime.
Not too many Christmases ago,
I heard about a man named Andrew
who was very ill himself,
but he had put on a Santa costume
each Christmas
for many years
to visit hospitalized children on Christmas Eve,
and he refused to let his last opportunity
to do this go by
without putting on that costume
one more time.
On Christmas Eve,
Andrew's wife and grown children
helped him into his Santa costume,
drove him to the hospital,
and helped him get to the pediatric ward.
Until the moment he stepped into the presence
of those hospitalized children

— some of them very, very sick —
Andrew was so weak himself
he could hardly walk.
But when he saw the faces of the children
he found energy and strength
he didn't know he had.
Andrew began to do his impersonation of me,
calling out, "Ho, ho, ho! Merry Christmas!"
to all the children.
Andrew had tears of love and joy
running down his cheeks,
and the children wondered
why Santa Claus was crying.
The little ones who could get out of bed
ran up to him and hung on his trousers.
Those confined to bed
held out their arms to him exclaiming,
"Santa! Santa Claus!"
Andrew went from bed to bed,
from one child to the next,
giving out small toys,
candy to those allowed to have it,
and every child got a big hug.
The Christmas joy Andrew brought
that Christmas Eve
was beyond measuring.

I, the real Santa Claus,
could not have done better myself.
On that Christmas Eve,
Andrew was more than
a Santa Claus impersonator.
In a genuine way,
he became me for those children.
When Andrew's family
got him home that evening,
he was the happiest of men.
The next day, on Christmas,
Andrew passed out of this world
into the realm of joy and light,
and he left behind a pediatric ward
full of children
who would never forget the Christmas Eve
when Santa Claus came to visit with them,
each and every one.
And do you know what?
The very next Christmas Eve
Andrew's oldest son, already a man himself,
put on his father's Santa costume
and carried on his father's tradition.

Three

What Christmas Means to Me

VERY YEAR
MANY PEOPLE WRITE AND SPEAK
ABOUT THE MYSTERY, JOY, AND DREAM
of Christmas.
Magazines publish hundreds
upon hundreds
of Christmas stories and articles.
Each year you find endless Christmas programs
on television and radio.
There are dozens of Christmas movies,
some of them with an actor
who impersonates me.
There are hundreds,
probably thousands of books
about Christmas.
You can find Christmas themes
on the World Wide Web,
or so my Executive Elf, Mistletoe, tells me...
In all of these ways

people make statements about
the meaning of Christmas.
Now it is my turn.
Now it is my turn to talk about the true meaning
of Christmas.
Perhaps you will be interested
to know what Santa Claus
thinks about Christmas.
That is the purpose of this part of my book,
to share with you my deepest beliefs
and convictions
about the mystery, joy, and dream
of Christmas.

The Religious Meaning of Christmas

As I said in the beginning,
everyone will agree that
there would be no Christmas
were it not for the birth of a Boy Child
in Bethlehem
some two thousand years ago.
It is true that for more than a few people
Christmas no longer has a religious meaning;
it is more of a winter festival,
and a time to be with family and friends.

I would say, however,
that for most people the religious character
and the sacred nature
of Christmas
still has meaning.
For me, personally,
this is also true.
For I am Santa Claus,
and Saint Nicholas is a big part of who I am.
Nicholas was a fourth-century Christian
priest and bishop
who later became a saint.
So how could I, Santa Claus,
not believe in the religious meaning
of Christmas?
If you are among those
who see no need
for this part of who I am,
I assure you that I am not offended.
I am Santa Claus,
and I am happy to contribute in any way
if it helps you and those you love
to find more joy in the Christmas
or winter holiday season.
All the same, I am Santa Claus,
and my soul comes from Saint Nicholas,

so I rejoice in the religious meaning of Christmas.
When you leave your homes
to attend Christmas worship services,
or attend a performance of Handel's *Messiah*,
I am there with you
in the back of the church or concert hall,
or off to one side,
someplace just out of view.
I am there,
and I pause with the children
in silent awe
to view the manger scene
Saint Francis of Assisi gave us
so many centuries ago.
In my own heart
I cannot separate Christmas
from that Boy Child born in Bethlehem
some two thousand years ago.
Because Father Nicholas,
who became Bishop Nicholas,
then Saint Nicholas,
is basic to who I am,
I believe that Boy Child
was the Child of the Divine Mystery,
and he came into the world
for love of us all.

I believe he came to bring healing,
forgiveness,
reconciliation,
freedom, and peace.
I believe he also came
to invite everyone to forget themselves
and remember the needs of others.
For me,
the religious meaning of Christmas
is a source of deep joy.
I know that apart from this meaning
Christmas would never be
what it is today,
even for those for whom
the religious character of Christmas
has little significance.
Christmas was born
among people who believed it to be
a celebration of healing,
forgiveness,
reconciliation,
freedom, and peace.
Christmas was born
among people who believed it to be
an invitation to forget themselves
and remember the needs of others.

Much of this same spirit survives today,
even among those for whom Christmas
is a secular winter festival.
But this would not be so
had it not been for the birth
of that Boy Child in Bethlehem
so very long ago.
I am Santa Claus,
I am Saint Nicholas,
and the religious meaning of Christmas
will always be close to my heart.

Christmas Is a Season of Miracles

If the many stories told about Christmas
agree on anything
it is this:
Christmas is a time to expect
miracles large and small.
I must tell you this:
Over the centuries
I have come almost to expect miracles
on Christmas.
In truth, I believe that
Christmas itself is a miracle.
Yes.

Christmas itself is a miracle.
What do I mean by this?
I mean that it is a miracle
that Christmas should happen at all,
that the Christmas spirit
should have as wide an impact as it does,
that the Christmas spirit
should touch as many hearts each year
as it does.
Each year we hear widespread grumbling
about how commercialized Christmas has become.
I must admit that this is true.
All the same,
even with all the buying and selling,
and talk about the bottom line,
and the gross national product,
here and there
the true Christmas spirit gets through.
Even in the most blatantly commercial situation,
where nothing but buying and selling
seems to happen,
the true Christmas spirit
often slips through.
A woman enters a department store.
She looks stressed out
from all her shopping.

A clerk approaches to help.
The clerk decided this year
to work at being a carrier
of the true spirit of Christmas.
So instead of thinking of the shopper
as just another hassle,
she looks at the shopper
as a human being,
someone who loves and is loved,
someone who has heartaches and joys,
someone who, deep down,
hungers for the true spirit of Christmas.
The clerk remarks to the woman
on how tired she must be,
even as she offers to help.
The shopper feels
the true spirit of Christmas.
It is a little bit of a miracle,
a Christmas miracle.
Christmas itself is a miracle,
the fact that it happens each year
is a miracle.
I don't mean to sound grim,
but compare the Christmas season
to any other time of the year.
What goes on the rest of the year?

For the most part,
people focus on their own lives,
their own goals,
their own projects.
Outside of people's own small circles of
home,
work,
and a few friends,
polite civility is about as good as it gets.
Then along comes Christmas.
At the darkest time of the year,
along comes Christmas,
and even the hardest of hearts
feels a tug in the other direction,
away from self
and toward others.
Even the hardest of hearts
opens up a bit more
to the possibility of joy.
The spirit of Christmas
has a widespread impact
not felt at any other time of the year,
and that is a miracle.
Sometimes, of course,
amazing miracles happen
on Christmas,

miracles of peace and reconciliation,
for example.
Everyone has heard the story
of the German and American troops
who faced one another across a battlefield
during World War I.
It was Christmas Eve,
and for no apparent reason
the enemies put aside their guns,
sang Christmas carols,
and embraced one another.
That was a Christmas miracle.

One of the most amazing
Christmas miracles I know of
happened in the early 1950s.
A man named John was a traveling salesman.
It was Christmas Eve,
and John was trying to make it home
to his family
through a snow storm and bitter cold.
He drove slowly
along an icy two-lane highway.

Suddenly, his car's engine stopped running,
and John realized he was out of gas.
In his hurry to get home,
he had forgotten to buy gasoline
in the last town he passed through.
As the car sputtered to a stop,
John began to pray,
asking God to send him some help.
Forty miles away,
his wife and two young children
were praying, too.
John knew that it would take a miracle
to get him home that night.
It would take a miracle
to keep him from freezing to death,
trapped in his car in a storm like that.
John prayed and waited,
hoping that help would arrive.
After about twenty minutes,
suddenly John saw headlights
approach from behind his car.
He got out and began to wave his arms.
The other car pulled to a stop,
and who should get out of the other car
but Santa Claus!
It was, of course,

a man impersonating me.
The Santa impersonator
asked John what the trouble was,
and John explained that he was out of gas.
"Santa" explained
that he was on his way
to a children's Christmas party
in the town where John lived.
He would give John a ride home.
John locked his car,
then climbed into the other man's car,
grateful that it had a good heater.
As they drove along, "Santa Claus"
introduced himself as Jake.
He said that each Christmas
he played Santa Claus
for various Christmas celebrations in the area.
He also served as the Santa Claus
for a couple of department stores,
so parents could bring their children
to tell Santa what they want for Christmas.
In about an hour,
Jake drove into the town where John lived
and delivered him
to the front door of his home.
John asked Jake to wait a moment.

He didn't tell Jake,
but John wanted to go into the house
and get Jake a few Christmas cookies
and a cup of hot chocolate
as a token of thanks.
While Jake waited in his car, the motor idling,
John went into the house,
embraced his wife and children,
and asked for some Christmas cookies
and a cup of hot chocolate
to give to the Good Samaritan Santa
who had rescued him from the storm.
The cookies wrapped in a paper napkin,
the hot chocolate in a paper cup,
John stepped back outside...
and Jake's car was nowhere to be seen.
The snow had stopped falling, the car was gone
...and there was no sign
a car had ever been there,
no tire tracks in the snow,
no sound of a car driving away in the distance.
Nothing.
John stood on his front porch,
his mouth open in amazement.
His wife came out
to ask what was the matter.

Where was the man
who had given John a ride home?
John turned to his wife,
smiled, gave her a kiss, and said,
"Merry Christmas. Have a cup of hot chocolate."
This was a Christmas miracle
they would never forget.
I can't tell you how many miracles
similar to this one
have happened over the years.
True stories like this
are one reason I believe
that Christmas is a season of miracles.

Christmas Is a Time for Family

Listen, now.
Here is one of my deepest convictions
about Christmas.
I believe with all my heart
that Christmas is a time for families
to be together.
Families nowadays are scattered
all over the map,
far and wide, wide and far,
sometimes even to distant parts of the earth.

But at Christmastime
everyone feels a tug
toward being with their family.
The airports and train and bus depots
are packed with people
headed home to be with family
for Christmas.
People often drive long distances.
This is good, this is as it should be.
People who have no family,
or people who are too distant from their families
to be with them,
such people want to be with friends,
people they care about
and who care about them.
For Christmas is a time
to be with those we love.
If we can't be with family
we do the best we can
to fashion for ourselves a family-like experience
for Christmas.
This is good, this desire to be with family
for Christmas.
As I have said before, however,
my name is Santa Claus,
not Pollyanna.

I realize that sometimes families
are hotbeds of conflict.
Sometimes family members don't get along
as well as they would like.
But no one should think
that love means the absence of conflict.
My goodness, no.
In his great nineteenth-century novel
The Brothers Karamazov,
Fyodor Dostoyevsky wrote:
"Active love is a harsh and fearful thing
compared to love in dreams."
We get along with some family members
like cats and dogs;
that is just the way it is,
and that does not mean
that we do not love one another.
Christmas is the best time of all
to remember our love for one another.
Christmas is the best time of all
for family members to say, "I'm sorry,"
to forgive past hurts,
to forgive and be reconciled.
For in the long run
what do we have that has more lasting value
than our family?

Friends may come and go,
but family remains.
Our family may get on our nerves sometimes,
but in the long run
they are all we have,
all we can count on
to be there for us
in good times and bad.
Christmas is the best time of all
to remember how important
our family is to us.

Christmas Is a Time for Giving

Everyone thinks of Christmas
as a time for giving gifts,
packages wrapped in brightly colored paper
and tied up with ribbons and bows.
So important has giving gifts become
that people sometimes refer
to the weeks before Christmas
as the "Shopping Season."
If anyone understands giving, it's me, of course.
That's my business every Christmas.
Sometimes I become concerned, however,
that many people today buy and give

brightly wrapped gifts
without understanding
the true spirit of Christmas giving.
For many people, buying and giving
has no purpose beyond itself.
Which is sad.
More and more children
think that Christmas
is about getting and getting,
stockpiling the latest "stuff."
What's frightening to me about this,
what keeps me awake nights,
in spite of good intentions all around,
is how a weird notion of love
gets blended into the mix.
Parents and grandparents,
for example,
often feel obligated
to buy children
the latest whiz-bangs and lolly-dockos
so the kids will feel loved.
So the kids will feel loved!
"If we do not buy them all this stuff,"
they say,
"the children will think
we do not love them."

Such people equate love
with the ability to spend piles of money
on whiz-bangs and lolly-dockos.
They believe they are
bad parents and grandparents
if they do not dump huge piles
of whiz-bangs and lolly-dockos
on the children.
So pervasive is this mixed-up perspective
that the kids believe it themselves.
If they do not get whiz-bangs and lolly-dockos
for Christmas
they feel unloved!
I am Santa Claus,
and even I don't know what to do
about this state of affairs.
I can only remind grownups
that even when children beg and plead
for whiz-bangs and lolly-dockos,
deep down what they want and need
more than anything else
is love.
Even if a child has a huge pile
of whiz-bangs and lolly-dockos
he or she will not, merely because of that,
feel loved deep down inside.

Even if parents and grandparents
have the financial resources
to buy children every one of the latest
whiz-bangs and lolly-dockos,
there are a few other things every child needs
more than anything else.
Now I'm talking about ideals here,
and I realize that most kids do not live
in ideal situations.
But I think we need to keep the ideals in mind,
all the same,
as something to aim for.

First, every child needs a father and mother
who are married to each other
and love each other.
This is the best gift
we can give our children.
I realize there are many single-parent families,
of course,
and most single parents do a wonderful job
of making a family and raising their children.
The important thing is to realize

that buying kids whiz-bangs and lolly-dockos
for Christmas
cannot compensate for an otherwise absent feeling
of love, warmth, and security.

Second, children need to learn
that the giving of gifts for Christmas
should be a sign and expression
of our love for one another,
not an attempt to substitute things for love.
Sometimes we have enough money
to spend on gifts,
but if we do not,
that should not get in the way
of showing our love at Christmas.
One of the best gifts, for example,
is the gift of time,
and the gift of time
is the gift of yourself.
Make or buy a Christmas card,
for example,
and write in the card a commitment
to spend a certain amount of time each week
with the child
in some activity the child will enjoy.
This is a Christmas gift

no one but you can give,
and you cannot buy it in any store.

Third, children must learn to give,
not just receive.
This can begin when a child is quite young.
Parents can ask:
What would you like to give
to your brother or sister?
To your friend?
There is no need for parents
to spend money on such gifts.
If the child has money
of his or her own to spend,
that's fine.
If not, ask what the child would like to make —
a card, picture, or craft project, for example.
Or help the child
to write a Christmas letter as a gift.
The important thing is for the child to learn
that Christmas is a time for giving.
We should receive gifts graciously and with joy,
of course.
But getting them is not very important.
I am Santa Claus, and I should know.

Four

Five Ways to Have a More Joyful Christmas

1. Bake Some Christmas Cookies

It is so easy to let Christmas happen to us.
It is so easy to let Christmas track us down
like a prowling animal
and pounce on us,
and knock us around, wham, wham, wham.
Wham.
It is so easy to let Christmas hit us
like a hit-and-run driver.
Wham.
Of course, when this happens
we claim we never saw it coming.
Of course, when this happens
it is not the true spirit of Christmas
that hits us.
Wham.
It is the false spirit of a phony Christmas
that hits us, wham.

If we seek the true spirit of Christmas,
if we want it to come into our life,
we must take certain steps.
We must take certain Christmas steps
to see to it that Christmas,
the true spirit of Christmas,
can find its way into our life.
We must take certain steps.
We must, for example,
bake some Christmas cookies.
We must, for example,
bake some Christmas fruitcake
or pumpkin bread.
Sounds too simple, I know.
But there is something
about baking something
for Christmas
that fills home and heart with the true spirit
of Christmas.
You need not be a prize-winning chef
to whip up a batch of Christmas cookies,
you know.
You need not have blue ribbons galore
from the county fair.
All you need is a recipe for Christmas cookies.
All you need do is follow the recipe.

All you need do is make this important enough,
make your desire for the true Christmas spirit
important enough
to make the time
to bake those cookies,
or that fruitcake or pumpkin bread.
And before you know it,
the true spirit of Christmas
will be in your heart.
Wham.

2. Go for a Christmas Walk

Each year,
after I return from my Christmas rounds,
I love to go for a walk.
All my work is done,
I am tired,
but there is one thing more I must do
before I go to sleep.
I must take my Christmas walk.
I walk,
I look at the early morning stars in the sky,
and I open my heart
to the true spirit of Christmas.
Think about going for a Christmas walk yourself.

The Truth About Christmas

Christmas Eve is a good time
for a Christmas walk.
Once your Christmas Eve events are over,
take a walk here or there.
If you live in a cold and snowy land,
put on your coat
and boots
and hat
and take a Christmas walk in the snow and cold.
Think about what Christmas means to you.
Think about Christmases past.
If you live in a warm or tropical land
—Hawaii, for example, or southern California—
go for a Christmas walk in the warm breezes
that make palm trees sway.
Think about the true meaning of Christmas
as you walk on Christmas Eve.
Some may prefer to walk on Christmas Day.
Either way,
go for a Christmas walk by yourself,
and open your heart
to the true spirit of Christmas.
Away from holiday noise, holiday clatter,
get in touch with the quiet, peace,
and simple joy
that is the true spirit of Christmas.

3. Listen Well to Christmas Music

During the holiday season
the air is filled with Christmas music.
Everywhere you go,
in the stores and in the streets,
you hear Christmas music
of all kinds.
Sometimes the Christmas music you hear
seems downright frantic.
It does not add to the true spirit of Christmas.
Instead, it seems to increase
the spirit of holiday chaos and uproar.
Bang, bang, bang,
more holiday clatter
amid the general holiday uproar.
Do not let it be.
Make sure to hear,
really listen to
some good Christmas music
sometime during the Christmas season.
Get yourself into a place
where you can breathe deeply,
quietly, calmly,
and prepare yourself to really listen
to some good Christmas music.

The Truth About Christmas

Live music is best.
If you can,
attend a performance of Handel's *Messiah*.
That would be good.
Sit there, forget the hectic exhaustion
of the season,
and soak in Handel's music.
If you look around,
you may find me there as well.
Let the music heal you
from the inside out.
If you cannot attend a live performance,
lay your hands on some good recordings.
Would you like to know a secret?
One of my all-time favorite recordings
of Christmas music
is by a group popular in the late 1950s
and early 1960s,
the Kingston Trio.
The Trio's utterly unique collection
of Christmas music,
The Last Month of the Year,
is, for me, timelessly beautiful,
entertaining, and uplifting.
Sometimes I listen to it
through earphones

on my portable compact disk player
as I fly through the night skies.
If you look you may find it yourself.
Of course, there are many other
beautiful recordings of Christmas music.
The key is to not let Christmas music
always be background music.
Instead, make time to sit down
and really listen to the music.
Listen, really listen.
Let Christmas music fill your heart
and help you to feel more deeply
the true spirit of Christmas.

4. Participate in Christmas Worship

I must tell you
that after many years of observation,
I have come to the conclusion
that as a merely secular winter holiday
Christmas has other ideas.
If Christmas is nothing more
than a winter festival,
a thinking person must ask,
"So what?"
and "Why bother?"

Why bother with the whole hectic business
if Christmas is nothing
but a winter festival
or merely a time to get together
with family and friends?
An honest person must ask,
"Is that all there is?"
On Christmas Eve,
or Christmas Day,
do as I do,
and attend Christmas worship services
someplace where you feel welcome.
I am Santa Claus,
and my heart comes from Saint Nicholas,
so for me Christmas would never be Christmas
unless I celebrate its religious meaning.
If this sounds strange to you,
take a deep breath
and give it a try.
Much Christmas joy
you may never have felt before
waits for you when you connect
with the religious meaning of Christmas.
Would Santa Claus,
who is Saint Nicholas,
mislead you about a thing like this?

5. Believe in Santa Claus

Christmas is a season for wonder,
a season for delight,
a season for joy,
and a reason to seek all three.
If you are an adult you must be on guard.
During the Christmas season
you must be on guard
against hardness of heart,
against cynicism,
against anything that would
deprive the Christmas season of its magic
for you.
So listen, listen,
listen to the sounds of Christmas,
especially in the night air of Christmas Eve.
Listen to the sounds of Christmas
and know that you can believe in me.
You can believe in Santa Claus
because I am as real as Christmas.
So here is the question:
"Is Christmas real for you?"
Do you find yourself struggling with
cynicism
and hardness of heart

125

when it comes to Christmas?
Determine that it shall not be so.
Determine to believe in me.

Listen.
The sleigh and the reindeer are waiting.
Come along with me.
The sleigh and the reindeer are waiting,
and Christmas is ready to be reborn
in your heart.
Come along with me.
The sleigh and the reindeer are waiting...